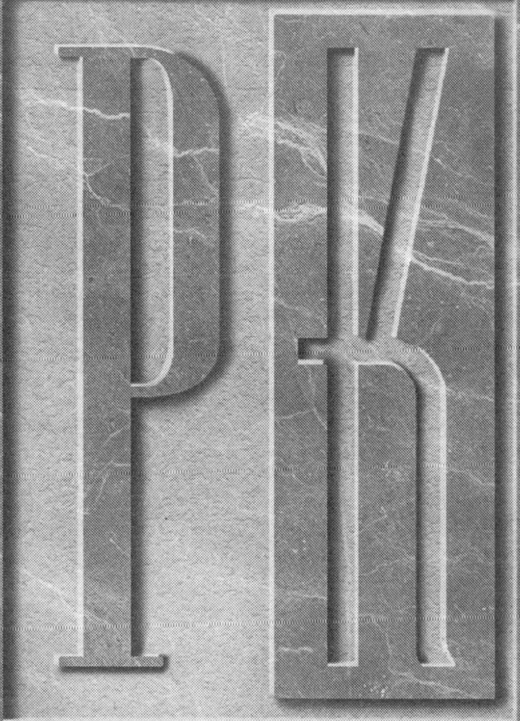

1998 OFFICIAL

SONGS FOR WORSHIP

LIVE A LEGACY

PROMISE KEEPERS '98

OFFICIAL SONGS FOR WORSHIP

LIVE A LEGACY

For More Information
About Promise Keepers Write To:
Promise Keepers
P.O. Box 103001
Denver, Colorado 80250
or call:
1.800.456.7594

COMPANION MATERIALS	
Cassette	080688580940
Compact Disc	080688589264
Songbook	080689301186
Singalong Book	3859711769
Split Tracks Accompaniment Cassette*	080689571145
Split Tracks Accompaniment CD*	080689569128

*The Cassette Trax and CD Trax are in the "Split-Trax" format (left channel, instrumental; right channel, vocals minus solos). The CD Trax provides maximum clarity and the truest music reproduction possible.

Edited by: Phil Kristianson and George Pavlov
Music Transcribed and Engraved by:
Bill Wolaver

Manufactured and Distributed by Word Music.
Printed by Davis Brothers Printing, Waco, Texas

PROMISE KEEPERS

We live in a world gone crazy, where a man's worth is gauged by the possessions he's gained. The corporate ladder, with all it's benefits, offers everything a man needs and a legacy to leave his children. "But what does it profit a man to gain the whole world and lose his own soul." In 1998, men from every walk of life will gather in stadiums and arenas to embrace the challenge to Live A Legacy of Christ in the world. The songs on this project will stir your heart to consider what you really value and what you want to be said about you when your life is over. Our families, friends, colleagues, and those who've gone before us are cheering us on as we run with patience the race set before us. Our great Savior Himself stands at the finish line to say well done. By His grace alone we stand. May these songs encourage you to be a vital part of the revival and awakening God is bringing to the earth today.

Rick Kingham
VP of Worship and Prayer

Dale Schlafer
VP for Revival and Awakening

TABLE OF CONTENTS

O God, Our Help in Ages Past

ISAAC WATTS

WILLIAM CROFT
Arranged by Tommy Walker

1. G C/G D/G
2. G C2/G G G/B
f
home! 2. Un - sure. O
15
D C G C/G G
God, You are, You are our help, You are our
f
C/G G D Dsus D C2 C
help - er; To all gen - er - a - tions You will be
G C/G G C/G G
23
D
for - ev - er and ev - er, Our Shield and our

C
G
D
F♯
Em
E - ter - nal Hope, O Lord. You are the
27
C C2
3
G
D
D
G
C
G
An - cient of Days and wor - thy of our praise.
G
G
B
rit.
C
Em
D
molto rit.
You are the An - cient of Days and wor - thy of our
rit.
molto rit.
G
34
Faster tempo
praise.

C/G G C/G G
mf
38
add cues: 2nd time
1. O God, our help in
God, our help in
C/G G Em A7 D
a - ges past, Our hope for years to come, Our
a - ges past, Our hope for years to come, Be
Em D C Gmaj7/B C D
shel - ter from the storm - y blast, And our e - ter - nal
Thou our guide while life shall last, And our e - ter - nal
1. G C/G G C/G G
home! 2. O
2. G C/G G C/G G
unis.
home. O

49
D
C
G
C/G
God, You are, You are our help, You are our
Am/G
G
unis.
help - er; To all gen - er - a - tions You will be
C/G
57
for - ev - er and ev - er, Our Shield and our
E - ter - nal Hope, O
D/F#
3rd time to Coda

Em
C
1. G/D
D
Lord. You are the An - cient of Days and wor - thy of our praise.
G
C/G
G
C/G
G
unis.
2. G/D
D
O wor - thy of our praise.
G
68
C
You are the An - cient of Days and
G/D
D
G
D.S. al CODA
unis.
wor - thy of our praise.
O

CODA
Em
73
C2
G/D
D
Lord. You are the An-cient of Days and wor - thy of our praise.
G
C/G
G
C/G
G
C2
You are the An-cient of Days and
G/D
D
G
C/G
G
C/G
G
wor - thy of our praise.
You are the
81
C
G/D
rit.
D
G
An-cient of Days and wor - thy of our praise.
rit.

For Such A Time As This

Words and Music by
PHIL KRISTIANSON, HOLLAND DAVIS,
MALCOLM DU PLESSIS, and RANDY ALWARD

we've been sum - moned here
Ah, for such a
we've been sum - moned here by God for
F/G
C7
Dm/C
C
15
time.
Hmm, will not,
such a time as this.
We will not be si -
B♭
F
B♭/C
F
we will not hold back.
- lent,
we will not hold back.
Cm7
F7
B♭

1.
SOLO in
Ah, for
Hmm,
By His grace we will rise up for such a time as this.
C
C9
B♭
F/A
Gm7
F
2.
For such a time, such a time.
For such a time as this.
B♭/C
B♭
F/A
Gm7
F
G
25
1. Through the mov - in' of His Spir - it, Hmm
(2.) make a dif - f'rence in our gen - er - a - tion, O yeah,
mp
Ooo,
Ooo,
Ooo,
C7
F
A♭/F
Gm/F

through
the mer - cy we do not de - serve,
ad - vance
His king - dom on ev - e - ry side;
Ooo,
Ooo,
F
G
C
C7
33
oh, yes.
We've been res -
uh huh,
To write his - to - ry
mf
Ooo
Ah,
F
F7
A
B♭
2nd time to Coda
- cued from ap - a - thy to
through our in - ter - ces - sion and
Ah
Bdim7
F
C
A7
C♯
Dm
A♭13

live the leg - a - cy of Christ in this world
Fmaj9/G
G7
B♭maj7/C
41
For such a time, for such a time,
(mel.)
For such a time as this, for
C
F
we've been sum - moned here
such a time as this, we've been sum - moned here
Gm7
F/G
Gm
Dm/G
C
Dm/C
C

Ah, for such a time as this. we will not,
by God for such a time as this.
B♭
F/A
Gm7
F
B♭/C
49
we will not, not hold back.
We will not be si - lent, we will not hold back.
F
Cm7
F7
B♭
But by His grace Ah, for
By His grace we will rise up for
C
C9

D.S. al CODA
such a time as this.
2. To
such a time as this.
B♭
F
A
Gm7
F
G
57
CODA
see thous - sands and thou - sands come to
Fmaj9
G
G7
f
Christ
For such a time,
f
For
B♭maj7
C
C
D
Am
D

61
SOLO: ad lib on repeat
Ah, for such a time as this,
such a time as this,
for such a time as this,
G
Am7
G/A
f
we've been sum-moned here by God,
Ah, for such
we've been sum - moned here by God for
Am7
G/A
Am
Em/A
D
Em/D
D7
3
69
a time.
And we will not,
such a time as this.
We will not be si -
C
G/B
Am7
G
C/D
G

Ah, we will not, but by His grace,
- lent, we will not hold back.
Dm7 G7 C
73
O, for
By His grace we will rise up for
D D9
1.
such a time. For such a time,
such a time as this.
C G/B Am7 G C/D
2.
such a time as this.
For such a time as this.
C G/B Am7 G

79
We will not,
O,
We will not be si - lent,
we will not hold back.
For by His grace we will
we will not hold back.
By His grace we will
Dm7
G7
C
D
Em
D
D7
rise up for such a time as this.
By His grace
rise up for such a time as this.
C
G
B
Am7
G
A7

87
for
By His grace we will rise up for
D
Em
D
D7
such a time as this.
Ooo, yes,
Ooo, yes,
such a time as this.
C
G
B
Am7
G
G
B
C
A
C♯
D
For such a time as this.
B
D♯
Em
Dm7
C7
B♭7
A7
A♭7
G7

Let It Rise

Words and Music by
HOLLAND DAVIS

10
E♭
songs of the Lord rise a-mong us, let the songs of the Lord
rise a-mong us, Let the joy of the King
A♭2
rise a-mong us, let it rise.
E♭
18
B♭
O,
A♭
let it rise.
E♭

B♭
A♭
O,
let it rise.
E♭
E♭2
26
E♭
(mel.)
Let the glo - ry of the Lord
rise a - mong us, let the glo - ry of the Lord
rise a-mong us, Let the prais - es of the King
A♭2

E♭
rise a - mong_ us, let it rise._
Let the
34
E♭
songs of_ the Lord_
rise a - mong_ us, let the
songs of_ the Lord_
rise a - mong_ us, Let the
A♭2
joy of_ the King_
rise a - mong_ us, let it rise._

E♭
42
B♭
O,
A♭
E♭
let it rise.
B♭
E♭
G
A♭
O,
let it rise.
E♭
f
Let the

50
F
glo - ry of the Lord
rise a - mong us,
let the
f
glo - ry of the Lord
rise a - mong us,
Let the
F
B♭
prais - es of the King
rise a - mong us,
let it rise.
F
Let the

58
F
songs of— the Lord—
rise
a - mong— us,
let the
songs of— the Lord—
rise
a - mong— us,
Let the
F
B♭
joy of— the King—
rise
a - mong— us,
let it rise.—
F

66
C
F
A
B♭
O,
let it rise.
1., 2., 3.
F
4.
Fsus
F
F2(no3)
F(no3)
Fsus
F
F2(no3)
F(no3)
Fsus
F
F2(no3)
F(no3)
F2(no3)

We Believe

Words and Music by
TODD WARREN

gath - er to kneel and to say that we are noth - ing
geth - er and of one race, that by Your blood,
A(no3)
with - out Your touch, O Lord. We
for You have cov - ered us. So to
E(no3)
15
say with one voice that we know that You are the God of
You we will sing and re - joice, we will of - fer this an - them of

all, and You will re - main for - ev - er on Your throne.
joy on and on, we will lift this song.
A(no3)
E(no3)
D
23
And we bow down,
And we bow down,
and we bow down.
We be -
and we bow, we bow down.
We be -
f
A(no3)
D
Bsus
B

27
E B E B E A
lieve in one Fa - ther, one Son and one Spir - it, we be - lieve in truth.
f
E B E B E B
Yes, we be - lieve in one Fa - ther, one Son and one Spir - it,
E A D
we be - lieve in truth; In the gos -
1. Bsus
36 E(no3) A(no3) D(no3)
- pel of Je - sus, we do.
mf

E(no3)
D(no3)
mf
2.
Bsus
2. In one
- pel of Je - sus, we do. —
E A D B
43
E B
We be - lieve in — one Fa - ther, one
f
E B E A E B
Son and — one Spir - it, we be - lieve — in truth. — Yes, we be -
E B E B
lieve in — one Fa - ther, one Son and — one Spir - it,

E
A
D
Bsus
we be - lieve in truth;
In the gos - pel of Je - sus, we do.
52
E(no3)
A(no3)
D(no3)
E(no3)
A(no3)
mf
We be - lieve,
D(no3)
E(no3)
A(no3)
Je - sus, we be - lieve.
D(no3)
E(no3)

Grace Alone

Words and Music by
SCOTT WESLEY BROWN
and JEFF NELSON

Dm7 Gsus G 15 C Csus/D C/E Am C/G G/F
is on-ly by His grace. Ev - 'ry moun - tain we will climb,
is on-ly by His grace. Ev - 'ry lov - ing word we say,
C Csus/D C/E F G Am F2(♯4) F
ev - 'ry ray of hopc we shine, Ev - 'ry bless - ing
ev - 'ry tear we wipe a - way, Ev - 'ry sor - row
C/E F2 Dm7 G7sus G7 C Csus/D C/E
mf
left be - hind is on - ly by His grace. Grace a -
turned to praise is on - ly by His grace.
23 F G2/B C Csus/D C/E F G2/B
lone which God sup - plies, strength un - known He will pro-
mf

C
Csus
D
C
E
F
E7
G♯
Am
C
G
vide,
Christ in us our Cor - ner - stone;
we will go
Dm11
G7sus
G7
1.
forth in grace a - lone.
Fmaj7
A
G2
B
G
B
2.
33
f
add cues: 2nd time
(mel.)
lone.
Grace a - lone which God sup - plies,
strength un -
known He will pro - vide,
Christ in us our Cor - ner -

1.
Am
C/G unis.
Dm7(4)
F/G
G7
C
C/E
stone; we will go forth in grace a - lone. Grace a -
2.
Am
C/G unis. mf
42
Dm7(4) rit.
F/G
G7
stone; we will go forth in grace a -
rit.
Am
Slower
C/G mp
Dm7(4)
F/G molto rit.
lone. We will go forth in grace a -
Slower
mp
molto rit.
C
Csus/D
C/E
Am
C/G
G7
C2
lone.

Stand Up, Stand Up for Jesus

GEORGE DUFFIELD, JR.

GEORGE J. WEBB
Arranged by Tommy Walker

A7
D7
G
G7/B
C
Am7
cross, Lift high His roy - al ban - ner, It
lone; The arm of flesh will fail you— Ye
G/D
D7
G
17
D
Am7
D
must not suf - fer loss; From vic - tory un - to
dare not trust your own; Put on the gos - pel
Em7
C
Em7
Am7
G/D
D
vic - tory His ar - my shall He lead, Till
ar - mor, Each piece put on with prayer; Where
G
G7/B
C
Am7
1. G/D
D7
ev - ery foe is van - quished And Christ is Lord in -
du - ty calls, or dan - ger, Be

G
G7/B
C
C/D
2. G/D
D7
deed.
2. Stand
nev - er want - ing
27
F2
C/E
G7
there.
Stand
31
up, stand up, stand — up,
Lift
up His ban - ner high.
Stand
up, stand up, stand — up,

F2
C/E
G7
Lift up His ban - ner high. 3. Stand
39
G
G7/B
C
Am7
G/D
Em7
up, stand up for Je - sus, The strife will not be
A7
D7
G
G7/B
C
Am7
long; This day the noise of bat - tle, The
G/D
D7
G
A7
47
D
Am7
D
next, the vic - tor's song;
(mel.)
To him that o - ver -

Em7
G7/D
C
Em7
Am7
G/D
D
come - eth A crown of life shall be; He
Am7/D
G/B
C
Am7
G/D
D7
with the King of glo - ry Shall reign e - ter - nal -
54
F2
C/E
G7
ly.
F2
C/E
G7
unis.
Stand

58
F2
C
E
G7
up, stand up, stand up, Lift
up His ban - ner high. Stand up, stand up, stand up,
Lift up His ban - ner high. Stand
66
up, stand up, stand up, Lift up His ban - ner high.
F

70
F2
C/E
G7
C/G
Stand up, stand up, stand up, Lift
up His ban - ner high.
1.
Stand
2.
Stand up, stand up, stand up,
Lift up His ban - ner high.

The Power of Your Love

Words and Music by
GEOFF BULLOCK

C
Dsus
D
Em7
grace that I found in You.
love as You live in me.
D
14
G
D
F♯
Em
And Lord, I've come to know the weak - ness - es I
Lord, re - new my mind as Your will un -
Bm7
Em
D
C
see in me will be stripped a - way,
folds in my life, in liv - ing ev - 'ry day,
C2
D
D
C
G
G
G
B
by the pow'r of Your love.
in the pow'r of Your love.

ALL unison: 1st time
add cues: 2nd time
22
f
C Em D Am/G
Hold me close, let Your love sur - round me;
G C Em D
Bring me near, draw me to Your
G
side.
30
C Em
And as I wait,
D Am/G G D/F♯
I'll rise up like the ea - gle, and I will soar with You,

34
Em
D
C
D
Your Spir - it leads me on in the pow'r of Your love.
1. C/G
G
2. C/G
G
C/G G
40
C
Em
D
(mel.)
Hold me close, let Your love sur -

Am/G
G
round me;
C
Em
D
C/G
G
Bring me near, draw me to Your side.
48
C
Em
D
G/D
Am/D
And as I wait, I'll rise up like the
Am/G
G
D/F♯
Em
ea - gle, and I will soar with You,

52
D
C
unis.
D
Your Spir - it leads me on
in the pow'r of Your love.
C/G
(SOLO may ad lib. to end)
1. G
D/F♯
Em
And I will soar with You,
2. Em
D
C
Em
rit.
D
C
And I will soar with You,
Your Spir - it leads me on
rit.
D
G
unis.
in the pow'r of Your love.

Who Is Like the Lord?

Words and Music by
HOLLAND DAVIS

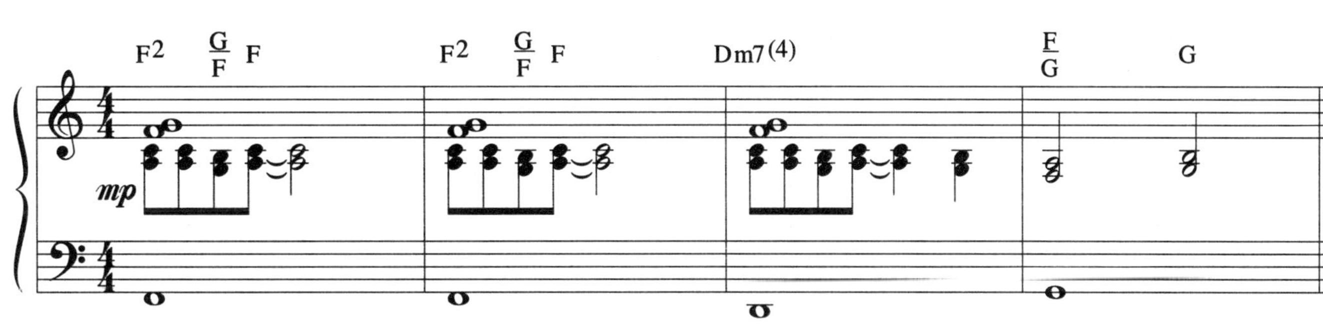

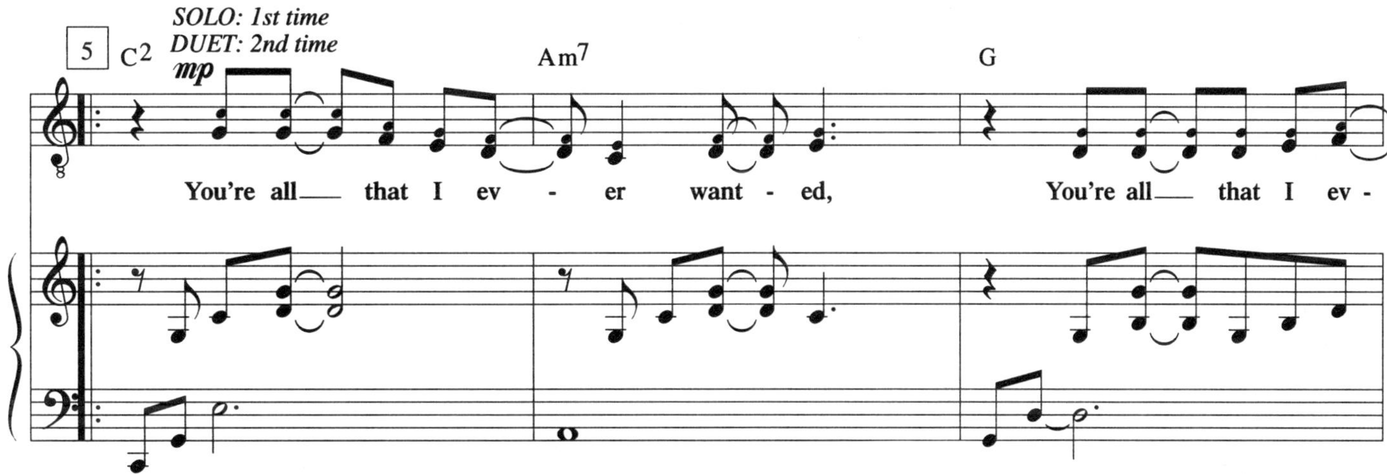

G
SOLO: both times
Dm7
E7
You were af - ter me. For Your love
13
Am
Em7
SOLO: both times
F
for me is e - ter - nal, and this I know is true,
G
C2
G/B
Am
SOLO: both times
I could nev - er re - pay the debt of
G
F2
G/F
F
F2
G/F
F
SOLO: 1st time
ALL unison: 2nd time
G
mf
love I owe to You.
For

22
C2
Am
Em
who is like the Lord, my God, com - pas - sion - ate and full
mf
G
C2
Am
of mer - cy? Who com - pares to Your great love? There's
G
Dm7/G
G/B
30
C2
none in all the earth. I will sing of Your love
Am
Em
G
and grace that cov - ers all my guilt and shame.

F2
G/F
F
F/G
G
F/G
G
1.
F
G/F
F
G/F
In all the earth who is like the Lord?
F
G/F
F
G/F
2.
C
C2
F2
G
(mel. in middle)
f
For
40
C2
Am
Em
who is like the Lord, my God, com - pas - sion - ate and full
f
G
C2
Am
of mer - cy? Who com - pares to Your great love? There's

G
Dm7/G
G/B
48
C2
none in all the earth.
I will sing of Your love
Am
Em
G
and gracc that cov-ers all my guilt and shame.
Fmaj9
G/F
Fmaj9
F/G
G
F/G
G
unis.
mf
In all the earth
who is like the Lord?
F
G/F
F
G/F
F/G
SOLO
rit.
G
F/G
G
C
Who is like the Lord?
rit.

Here I Am

Words and Music by
BILL BATSTONE

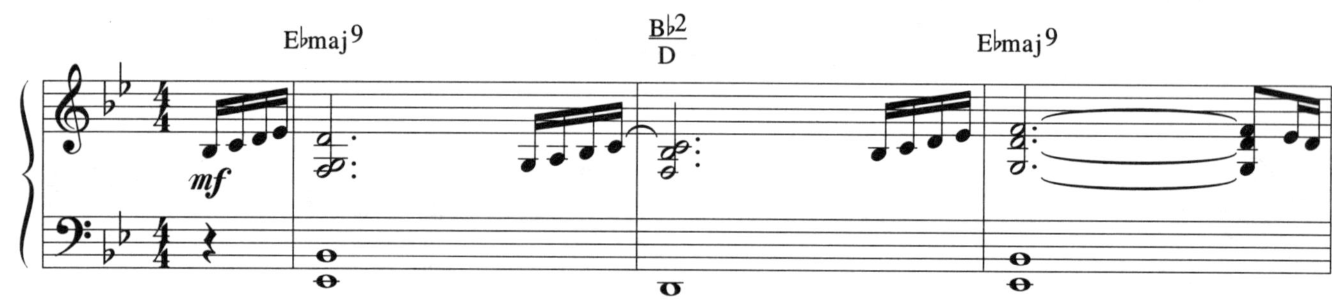

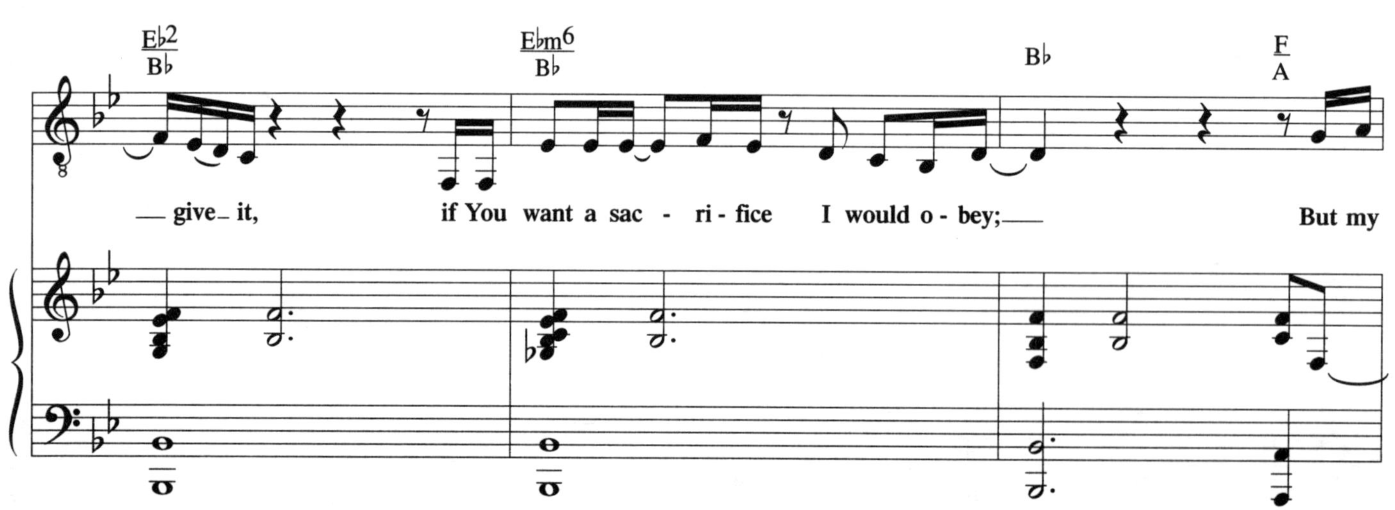

Gm7
C2
life is all I have and I will live it ded - i -
Ebmaj9
Fsus
F
cat - ed to the hon - or of Your name.
13
Bb
Eb2/Bb
Glad - ly will I bow down as Your serv - ant,
Ebm2/Bb
Bb(no3)
F/A
glad - ly will I wait for Your com - mand. I com-

Gm7
C2
E
mit my trust to You for You de - serve it, I de -
E♭maj9
Fsus
F
ALL unison
mf
light with - in the guid - ance of Your hand.
Here I
21
SOLO
am and I long to do Your will, here I
add cues: 2nd time
am and I long to do Your will, here I
B♭
E♭
B♭
mf

am, I'll fol - low Your com - mand. Here I am, Lord,
am, I'll fol - low Your com - mand. Here I
F/A F B♭ F/A
25
un - til my call - ing is ful - filled, here I am,
am un - til my call - ing is ful - filled, here I
Gm7 Cm7
2nd time to Coda
Lord, here I am, Hmm, yeah. For
am, here I am.
Fsus F B♭ E♭2/B♭

30
SOLO
mp
B♭
E♭2/B♭
You have placed Your ho - ly Word with - in me, Your
E♭m2/B♭
B♭(no3)
F/A
book of truth is liv - ing in my heart.
Gm7
C2/E
Writ - ten on each page from the be - gin - ning there's a
E♭maj9
Fsus
F
ALL
mf
D.S. al CODA
(mel.)
call for me to play my part. Here I

CODA
am. Here I am, Hmm, here I am.
unis.
am. Here I am, here I am.
Gm7 F/G Gm7 Cm7 F G♭ G♭/A♭ A♭
41
D♭
SOLO
mf
G♭/D♭
A♭/D♭
Lord, I have sung Your praise,
D♭
G♭/D♭
A♭/C
I've lift - ed up Your name!

45
B♭m
E♭m7
F7(♭9)
I've told the con - gre - ga - tion, Lord,
B♭m
E♭m7
E♭m
C
F
of Your great sal - va - tion,
Lord,
Here I
N.C.
E♭
F

51
SOLO: ad lib. on repeat
am, here I am, Lord. Here I am,
am and I long to do Your will, here I
B♭
E♭/B♭
f
I'll fol - low Your com - mand. Here I am, Lord.
am, I'll fol - low Your com - mand. Here I
F/A
F
B♭
F/A
Ooo, yeah, un - til my call - ing is ful - filled, here I
am un - til my call - ing is ful - filled, here I
Gm7
Cm7

1.
2.
am, Lord, here I am. Here I am. am, Je - sus, here I
am, here I am. Here I am, here I
Fsus F B♭ E♭/F Fsus F
mf
rit.
62
Slower
am. Here I am, here I am,
am. Here I am, here I am.
unis.
Gm Gm/F Cm7 Fsus F E♭maj9
molto rit.
freely
3
here I am, here I am.
B♭2/D Cm7(4) Fsus F B♭2

Instruments of Your Peace

Words and Music by
KIRK DEARMAN
and DEBY DEARMAN

A
B
E
A2
of Your peace, walls of pride and prej - u - dice shall
Bsus
B
1.
F♯m7
E/G♯
A
B
E
A/E
E
cease when we are Your in - stru - ments of peace.
2., 3.
F♯m7
E/G♯
A
B
E
A/E
E
when we are Your in - stru - ments of peace.
15
SOLO
E
B
E
1. Where there is ha - tred we will sow His love,
2. Where there is blind - ness we will pray for sight,

cues: 2nd time
where there is in - ju - ry
where there is dark - ness
we will nev - er judge.
we will shine His light.
19
E
B
E
Where there is striv - ing
Where there is sad - ness
we will speak His peace
we will bear their grief,
2nd time to Coda
A2
Bsus
B
to the peo - ple cry - ing for re - lease,
to the mil - lions cry - ing for re - lease
D.S. al CODA
A2
Bsus
B
E
we will be His in - stru - ments of peace.

CODA
A2
Bsus
B
E
we will be His in - stru - ments of peace.
27
ALL: both times
(SOLO may ad lib. 2nd time)
(mel. in middle)
E
A
B
E
Lord, make us in - stru - ments of Your peace,
B
A
Bsus
B
where there is ha - tred let Your love in - crease;
E
A
B
E
Lord, make us in - stru - ments of Your peace,

A2
Bsus
B
walls of pride and prej - u - dice shall cease
F♯m7
E
G♯
A
B
1. E
when we are Your in - stru - ments of peace.
2. E
38
A2
Bsus
B
peace.
When we are Your in - stru - ments of
C♯m7
F♯m7
E
G♯
A
B
E2
unis.
molto rit.
peace.
When we are Your in - stru - ments of peace.
molto rit.